OVERCOMING DIVISIVENESS

Lessons from Emanuel Swedenborg

D0815064

Text by EMANUEL SWEDENBORG

Passages selected and reflections written by MORGAN BEARD

SWEDENBORG
FOUNDATION
West Chester, Pennsylvania

Library of Congress Cataloging-in-Publication Data

Names: Swedenborg, Emanuel, 1688-1772, author. | Beard, Morgan, author.
Title: Overcoming divisiveness : lessons from Emanuel Swedenborg / text by
    Emanuel Swedenborg ; passages selected & reflections written by Morgan Beard.
Description: West Chester, Pennsylvania : Swedenborg Foundation, [2021] |
    Summary: "As long as there have been groups of people, there have been divisions
    between them-personal, ideological, racial, religious, ethnic, and more. The
    ideological divisions in society, particularly those in American society, have been the
    subject of a lot of discussion in recent years, and at times the divide between the
    various camps seems insurmountable. This short work contains a series of passages
    on division and conflict from the writings of Emanuel Swedenborg. Each passage
    is accompanied by a summary of key points and questions to discuss or ponder
    privately, giving readers the opportunity to dig deeper into a unique system of
    spiritual introspection and growth"—Provided by publisher.
Identifiers: LCCN 2020052015 | ISBN 9780877854326 (paperback) |
    ISBN 9780877857136 (epub)
Subjects: LCSH: New Jerusalem Church--Doctrines.
Classification: LCC BX8711.A7 B43 2021 | DDC 230/.94--dc23
LC record available at https://lccn.loc.gov/2020052015

Design and typesetting by Karen Connor
Printed in the United States of America

Swedenborg Foundation
320 North Church Street
West Chester, PA 19380
www.swedenborg.com

Dedication

This book is dedicated to the memory of Hyland Johns, a long-time friend and supporter of the Swedenborg Foundation. Without his encouragement and his love for this topic, you wouldn't be reading this book today.

ooooo

Contents

Introduction

As long as there have been groups of people, there have been divisions between us—personal, ideological, racial, religious, ethnic, every type you can imagine. In the United States, the ideological divides have become so deep and entrenched that it's become hard to imagine any type of reconciliation between the two sides. But divisiveness doesn't have to be founded in politics; personal conflicts of all types—at home, among friends and family, in workplaces—can be a source of pain and anxiety for anyone.

This book offers thoughts from the writings of Emanuel Swedenborg (1688–1772) that give insights into the roots of interpersonal conflict and perspectives on how to overcome them. Swedenborg was a Swedish scientist and mystic who had a series of spiritual experiences in his mid-fifties that led to a radical transformation in his life. His visions of the spiritual world—of conversations with angels, devils, and the spirits of people who had crossed over—were so powerful that he was compelled to share what he had learned, writing twenty-five volumes of spiritual commentary on subjects ranging from biblical commentary to the nature of God and divine providence. Although the social situations in the time and place where he lived were much different from ours, his books describe a system of spiritual growth that remains profoundly relevant today. You can learn more about his life in the biography at the end of the main text.

In this book, passages from Swedenborg's works are collected by theme in each chapter. Following each passage, you'll find the core idea expressed in that passage along with a short description of what it entails, as well as questions for discussion or reflection that are intended to help illustrate how that concept can be directly and meaningfully applied to daily life. You are invited to read the passages from Swedenborg when you need inspiration, use the quotes and reflections as a starting point for a group discussion, or simply enjoy the material as food for your own spiritual journey. You might also find the passages to be inspiration for your own prayers, meditations, creative works, or other techniques for connecting with the Divine.

This book was originally written as one in a series of free books created annually for members of the Swedenborg Foundation, and is now being offered for sale because of the overwhelmingly positive response. Most of the content is the same as the membership edition, but for this new release we've added a bonus chapter, "The Words We Use."

The quotes in this book are all taken from the New Century Edition of the Works of Emanuel Swedenborg, a translation of his writings published by the Swedenborg Foundation. Sources are cited by paragraph number rather than by page number so that you can cross-reference passages in any translation of Swedenborg's writings. You can also download any one of his theological works for free at www.swedenborg.com.

I hope this book helps you in your personal journey!

Morgan Beard
Executive Director, Swedenborg Foundation
West Chester, Pennsylvania

ooooo

THE TYPES OF LOVE

What we love—the thing that drives us—is the root of all conflict. In this chapter, we take a look at the different types of love and the ways in which a self-centered love can lead to divisions between us.

We have as our goal whatever we love more than anything else. This is what we focus on overall and in every detail. It is within our will like the hidden current of a river that draws and carries us along even when we are doing something else, because it is what animates us.

What is loved above all is also something we look for and see in others, and something we use to influence them or to cooperate with them.

The way we are is entirely determined by what controls our life. This is what distinguishes us from each other. This is what determines our heaven if we are good and our hell if we are evil. It is our essential will, our self, and our nature. In fact, it is the underlying reality of our life. It cannot be changed after death because it is what we really are.

— *New Jerusalem* 56–57

Key Concept

What we love is the core of our identity; it determines everything about who we are. If you're wondering what this has to do with divisiveness, take another look at the second paragraph: "What is loved above all is also something we look for and see in others." In other words, the way we relate to other people is determined, first and foremost, by what we ourselves most value.

For Discussion or Reflection

What do you love more than anything else? The answer might be a specific person or thing, or it might even be an idea or principle. Now, take a step back to think about what that love represents. For example, maybe what you love above all else is family. What does family mean to you? What are the qualities that you love most about family?

Think about the kinds of things you look for in others. When you meet someone new, what do you ask them about? What types of things make you think better or worse of a person? Based on your answers to these questions, would you say that what you look for in others relates to what you value most?

There are two kinds of love that generate all that is good and true, and two kinds of love that generate all that is evil and false. The two kinds of love that are the source of everything good and true are love for the Lord and love for our neighbor; the two kinds of love that are the source of everything evil and false are love for ourselves and love for this world.

— *New Jerusalem* 59

Key Concept

Swedenborg has quite a bit to say about these four different kinds of love (see, for example, *New Jerusalem* 54–61, 65–80, and 84–105), but to sum up:

- Love for the Lord is exactly what it sounds like: love of all things divine.
- Love for our neighbor is a love for others (regardless of where they live) and a willingness to put their good above our own.
- Love for ourselves is meant not in the positive sense of having self-esteem. Instead, it is meant in the negative sense of putting our own good before anyone else's.
- Love for the world, too, is meant in its negative sense: loving such things of this world as money, power, material goods, fame, and so on.

As we shall see, it's the second two loves that get us into trouble.

For Discussion or Reflection

Can you think of examples in your own life of each of these four different types of love? How does each of them affect how you behave?

How do you see other people exhibiting each of these four loves? How do you react to the different types of behavior that they demonstrate?

The evil qualities generally found in people who love themselves are contempt for others, jealousy, unfriendliness toward people who do not favor them; a resulting hostility; and various kinds of hatred, vengefulness, guile, deceit, ruthlessness, and cruelty. Where you find evils like this, you also find contempt for God and for the divine things that are the true insights and good actions taught by the church . . . .

Love for the world, on the other hand, is wanting to redirect other people's wealth to ourselves with whatever skill we have. It is putting our heart in riches and letting the world distract us and steer us away from spiritual love (love for our neighbor) and heaven. We have a love for the world if we long to redirect other people's possessions to ourselves by various methods, especially if we use trickery and deception, and have no concern for how our neighbor is doing. If we have this type of love, we have a strong and growing craving for good things other people have. Provided we do not fear the law or losing our reputation, we take people's things away, and in fact rob people blind.

— *True Christianity* 400:10–11

Key Concept

Here, Swedenborg describes how love for ourselves and love for the world can express themselves in such attitudes and behaviors as rage, selfishness, and vengefulness. The more we focus on ourselves and on what we can gain from others, the more we put ourselves on a pedestal and begin to truly believe that our desires are all that matter. And the more we try to protect this sense of self-importance, the more that we act out in ways that are hurtful or even harmful.

For Discussion or Reflection

Do you know people who regularly exhibit any of the above qualities? If so, have you ever come into conflict with them? What was the result? Would you do anything differently if something like that were to happen to you again?

What do you think causes people to behave in these ways?

Can you think of a situation in which a little bit of love for oneself or love for the world could be a beneficial thing?

What is higher or lower rank; what is more or less wealth? Is it really anything but something we imagine? Is one person more contented or happier than the other? Look at a government official or even a monarch or emperor. After a few years, does their rank not become simply commonplace, something that no longer brings joy to the heart, something that can even seem worthless? Are people of high rank any happier on that account than people of lower rank, or even than people of no rank at all, like commoners or their servants? These can be even happier when things go well for them and they are content with their lot. What troubles the heart more, what is more often wounded, what is more intensely angered, than self-love? This happens whenever it is not given the respect to which, at heart, it raises itself, whenever things do not turn out the way it wills and wishes.

— *Divine Providence* 250:2

Key Concept

Here, we see the trap of love for ourselves and love for the world: People never achieve happiness through self-gratification, wealth, status, or other such means. No matter what they achieve, it's only temporary; by focusing on material success, they miss the true prize: peace of mind. And the more that they try to build their happiness on their own self-importance, the more painful it is whenever that sense of importance is threatened.

For Discussion or Reflection

What makes you happy? Or, to look at it another way, what do you do when you want to feel happy? Thinking about happiness in the context of the different types of love, why do you think the source of your happiness makes you feel the way you do?

Do you know others who strike you as particularly happy people? Why do you think they are happy? Would it surprise you if you found out that they actually aren't happy at all? If so, why?

All selfishness and materialism—which are matters of human will—are simply forms of hatred, because the more we love ourselves the more we hate our neighbor. Since love for ourselves and love of worldly gain are therefore opposed to heavenly love, they necessarily pour out a constant stream of impulses that go against mutual love.

— *Secrets of Heaven* 1047

Key Concept

We've seen in the previous sections how selfishness and materialism can lead to all types of negative attitudes and behaviors. When taken to the extreme, though, they can cause a person to become outright hateful. As Swedenborg says here, they are in fact "forms of hatred" themselves since there is a direct relationship between our self-love and our hatred toward others. So we're left with a proposition to ponder: any hatred that lives within us, however small, might be a product of our love for ourselves and therefore be the root of our conflicts.

For Discussion or Reflection

It's easy to see how selfishness can lead to certain kinds of conflict—a person acting petty and making other people's lives difficult, for example—but how does it relate to an argument where both sides genuinely believe they're acting for the good of others? How does love for ourselves enter into broader social issues like immigration or abortion? How might other types of love come into play in those debates?

Do you agree with the proposition that the more we love ourselves, the more we hate others? Why or why not?

People may judge for themselves what they would be like . . . if they were allowed to behave with no fear of the law or fear for their lives, without any outward restraints—threats to their reputation or to their rank, their profit, and the pleasures that attend them.

— *Heaven and Hell* 508:5

Key Concept

This idea has been the inspiration for all types of popular fiction, from *The Lord of the Flies* to the movie series *The Purge*. How would we act if there was nothing to stop us from doing whatever we wanted and there were no consequences to our actions? Swedenborg argues that we would engage in every type of horrible behavior imaginable—unless we were to begin going down the path of spiritual growth.

For Discussion or Reflection

How do you think *you* would behave if there were no consequences to your actions and nothing to prevent you from doing whatever you liked?

What do you think society as a whole would be like if these were the conditions?

Do you think that living in this way would make you freer than you are right now? Why or why not?

THE EFFECTS OF HATE

We've all seen the toxic effects that hatred of others can have on a person, but Swedenborg tells us that there are spiritual consequences as well—including some we might not expect.

If we despise our neighbors or regard people as our enemies for merely disagreeing with us or not showing us reverence or respect, our life is a life of self-love. If for similar slights we hate our neighbors and persecute them, then we are even more deeply entrenched in self-love. And if we burn with vengeance against them and crave their destruction, our self-love is stronger still; people with this attitude eventually love being cruel.

— *New Jerusalem* 68

Key Concept

Here, Swedenborg shows the progression of self-love: It can start with a seed as small as a minor disagreement, but if we let it fester, it keeps growing. Maybe we start to generalize about the person and say, "He does this all the time," or "You just can't reason with her!" Over time, what started as a minor issue becomes a bitter anger and resentment. And once we start thinking of someone who disagrees with us as "the enemy" and are even inclined to do them harm, it becomes easier to start thinking that way about other people, too. The downward spiral becomes more and more difficult to reverse.

For Discussion or Reflection

Have you ever been part of an argument that spiraled out of control? If so, how did it end? Or are those feelings still unresolved?

If you like, try an exercise: The next time you have a difference of opinion with someone, see if you can pay attention to your thoughts and feelings as they are happening. What kinds of thoughts are you having about that person? What kinds of emotions do those thoughts evoke? Where do those thoughts and feelings lead?

If we believe that particular evils are permissible, then they do become part of us even though we do not do them, since the permission we grant them in our thought comes from our intent, and there is an agreement. As a result, when we believe that some particular evil is permissible, we have relaxed the inner restraint against it and are kept from doing it only by outward restraints, which are fears.

— *Divine Providence* 81

Key Concept

This is another important concept about love and hate: whatever we accept as true in our mind becomes a part of us. In this case, Swedenborg is talking about evil behavior, and he says that even believing that particular behaviors are all right is the same as doing them.

We can apply this concept to the hateful attitudes described in previous passages (see, for example, page 6). If we say to ourselves that there's nothing wrong with getting revenge on someone who wronged us, or getting angry with a person who does this or that, then we make revenge and anger parts of ourselves.

For Discussion or Reflection

Think about a conflict that you've witnessed between two parties. Did you have strong feelings about what was said? If so, what was the nature of those feelings? Did you side with one or the other party, either out loud or in your thoughts? What were the values (that is, the loves) that led you to feel or act that way?

Are there things that might be considered illegal, immoral, or harmful to others that you feel are allowable? If so, why? Would you do them, given the opportunity?

[If he had not given permission for evils to happen], the Lord could not lead us out of our evil, so we could not be reformed and saved. That is, unless evils were allowed to surface, we would not see them and therefore would not admit to them; so we could not be induced to resist them. That is why evils cannot be suppressed by some exercise of divine providence. If they were, they would stay closed in, and like the diseases called cancer and gangrene, would spread and devour everything that is alive and human.

From birth, each of us is like a little hell in constant conflict with heaven. The Lord cannot rescue any of us from our hell unless we see that we are in it and want to be rescued. This cannot happen unless there are instances of permission that are caused by laws of divine providence.

This is why there are lesser and greater wars, the lesser ones between property owners and their neighbors and the greater ones between the rulers of nations and their neighbors. The only difference between the lesser and the greater ones is that the lesser ones are limited by national laws and the greater ones by international laws.

— *Divine Providence* 251:1–2

Key Concept

One of the ways in which God shows us what evil looks like is through larger open conflicts like wars. By witnessing firsthand the massive suffering caused by war, we understand better the cost of pursuing our own agenda of self-promotion and power. Likewise, on a more local level, witnessing or being part of a smaller-scale battle helps us to understand the consequences of indulging in negative emotions.

For Discussion or Reflection

Have you ever been involved in a war—either in the literal sense of a large-scale military conflict or in the figurative sense of a particularly nasty fight between two parties? Or, if you haven't taken part in one, have you witnessed one? If so, did it change the way you think about fighting? How?

What are your thoughts on the statement that "evils cannot be suppressed by some exercise of divine providence"? In what ways might it play a part in how we consider our actions and intentions?

Wicked and loathsome acts—that is, acts of hatred—are what turn us away and make us look downward only, toward bodily and earthly concerns, or in other words toward the things of hell. This happens when we send charity into exile and extinguish it, which shatters the bond between the Lord and us. Only charity, which is love and mercy, maintains the bond.

— Secrets of Heaven 379

Key Concept

Let's start with a definition: When Swedenborg writes about charity, he's not talking about the act of giving money to a good cause; he's talking about a sense of love or goodwill toward others, in the same sense as "love for our neighbor."

Here, then, we see an even more intense degree of self-love: when we become so self-involved that we turn our backs on charity, we lose our connection to the Lord. And without that connection, we become more prone to committing acts of hatred.

For Discussion or Reflection

Have you ever committed an act that could be considered "wicked and loathsome"? If so, how did you feel while you were doing it? How did you feel afterward? Do you agree with Swedenborg's statement that such acts turn us toward hell?

Think about a time when you were angry with someone—not just annoyed, but absolutely raging. Was there any room in that experience for love to enter? If so, and you were able to think about loving that person, what happened? If love was the furthest thing from your experience, what do you imagine would have happened if you had tried to think about loving them?

The Lord shows mercy to everyone, loves everyone, and wants to make everyone happy forever. As a result, those who lack sufficient love to have mercy on others, love them, and want to make them happy cannot unite with the Lord, because they are unlike him and are anything but his image. To gaze at the Lord through the lens of supposed faith and yet hate others is not only to stand far removed from the Lord, it is also to put a deep, hellish gulf between yourself and the Lord, a gulf you will fall into if you try to approach him. Hatred for other people is that intervening, hellish chasm.

— *Secrets of Heaven* 904:2

Key Concept

Here, Swedenborg elaborates on the theme from the previous passage: those who are unable to show love for their neighbor put an unbridgeable gulf between themselves and the Divine. Love cannot harmoniously coexist with hate. Even though as human beings we are usually a mix of these two, Swedenborg tells us that eventually one love will win out over all the rest, whether it happens in earthly life or in the afterlife.

For Discussion or Reflection

Thinking back on all the examples of hate that we discussed in previous passages, do you see instances of this type of self-love or love for the world in yourself? How do you react to the idea that having such emotions can keep you apart from the Lord?

Whatever we have done during bodily life, and even whatever we have thought, gradually comes back in the other life. When the hostile, spiteful, underhanded actions we have taken return, the individuals we hated and secretly plotted against also appear before us, and appear in an instant. That is how things operate in the next life. . . . The negative thoughts we have had about the people are also plain to see, since everyone's thoughts are perceptible. Miserable states result; hidden hatreds erupt openly.

Bad people find that all their misdeeds and thoughts come back with vivid realism in this way, but good people do not. With them, all states of goodness, friendship, and love return, bringing with them the highest pleasure and happiness.

— *Secrets of Heaven* 823

Key Concept

Swedenborg teaches that what we love shapes not only our life on earth but also our afterlife in the spiritual world. This doesn't mean that we spend eternity reliving every little mistake we've made—the actions that come back to us are the ones that we believed were justified, and they are therefore made a part of our spiritual selves. Those conscious choices have lasting effects (see page 18), and we have to face them in order to achieve peace.

For Discussion or Reflection

If you were to die today, what do you think you would find in the afterlife? Who would appear in front of you, and what might you say to each other?

Think about someone you've clashed with here on earth. Would it change the way you interacted if you could read each other's thoughts? In what way?

THE WORDS WE USE

Sometimes our attempts to communicate can be a source of misunderstanding and division—especially in online forums, where emotions can run high and it's easy to react quickly or impulsively. Swedenborg offers wisdom about how to look beneath the surface of words to see the emotions and intentions beneath.

The angel from the heaven of wisdom asked the other angel, "What is love?"

The other angel replied, "The love that originates from the Lord as a sun is the vital heat that angels and people have—it is the underlying reality of their lives. The derivatives of love are called feelings. Feelings produce perceptions and therefore thoughts. It flows from this that wisdom starts out as love, and therefore thought starts out as the feeling related to that love. Looking at the derivatives in sequence makes it possible to see that thought is nothing but the form of the feeling. This is not generally known, because thoughts exist in light but feelings exist in heat, and therefore people reflect on their thoughts but not on their feelings. . . .

"This point would become crystal clear if someone were to say, 'Take the sound out of your speech.' Would there be any speech left? Also, 'Take the feeling out of your thinking.' Would there be any thinking left?"

—*True Christianity* 386:2

Key Concept

Here Swedenborg lays out a progression: The life within us starts as love streaming out from God. But as it enters us and then re-emerges into the world through our actions, that love changes—like light through a prism—and becomes something unique to who we are. What we love as individuals—the overriding love that shapes our core identity—in turn shapes how we feel, and what we feel shapes how we think.

That might seem counterintuitive if you're used to thinking about thoughts as rooted in reason. But in this passage, the message is that our emotions drive us more than we realize, so our underlying values may drive our actions in ways that we don't always recognize consciously.

For Discussion or Reflection

Recall an argument that you had, or consider a political or social issue that generates strong emotions for you. Now sit with the emotions associated with these thoughts, whether they be anger, fear, or something similar. Where are the emotions coming from? If it's not immediately clear, take some time to trace them back to their source. What is the love behind them?

Angels recognize our love from the sound of our speech, our wisdom from the way the sound is articulated, and our knowledge from the meaning of the words. They also tell me that these three elements are in every word, because a word is like a realization that has the sound, the articulation, and the meaning within it. Angels of the third heaven have told me that they sense from any word a speaker says in a sentence the general state of that individual's mind, and some specific states as well.

—*Divine Love and Wisdom* 280

Key Concept

Swedenborg describes the spiritual world as a place where all our thoughts and feelings are revealed for everyone to see. Of course, here on earth, things are quite different, but we can still tell a lot from such nonverbal cues as facial expression and tone of voice. In writing, the words that people choose and the way they express their ideas can even reveal quite a bit about where they're coming from.

For Discussion or Reflection

Have you ever received a message—either verbally or in writing—that felt extremely divisive? How do you think an angel would perceive those same words? In what way(s) would an angel hear them differently, and what might be revealed to them in doing so?

How would an angel perceive your response to that message?

I have been told by angels that on every planet the very first form of speech has been facial, using the two basic means of the lips and the eyes. The reason this kind of speech comes first is that the face has been formed to reflect what we think and what we want. That is why the face is called the image and index of the mind. It is also because honesty was a characteristic of the earliest or primal times. People did not have thoughts, and did not want to have thoughts, that they were unwilling to show in their faces. This allowed the feelings of their minds and their consequent thoughts to be vividly and fully presented in their faces. So their thoughts and feelings were visible to others' eyes in a single form containing many details at once. This kind of speech therefore surpassed verbal speech the way seeing something surpasses hearing about it—for example, seeing a field for yourself as opposed to hearing and understanding a verbal description of it.

—*Other Planets* 54:2

Key Concept

When Swedenborg writes about the first people on earth, he always describes them as being closest to the divine. Like angels, these people simply allowed their faces to express everything in their mind without worrying about others think. But, also like angels, it was easy for them to do so, because they were so full of divine love that there was nothing to be embarrassed about. We could also think of that state as childlike: the innocence of not saying anything other than what's on our mind.

For Discussion or Reflection

Have you ever gone through an entire day without telling a lie? Sometimes it's even as small as answering "fine" when someone asks you how you are, even if you're not feeling fine at all. If you like, try this as a conscious exercise: for a period of time (a day, a week), notice how often you tell the truth and how often you lie. What are the situations when you speak truthfully, and what are the situations when you don't?

There's also another aspect to truth-telling: not just telling the truth, but saying what's really on your mind, regardless of the circumstances or how you think it might be perceived. Have you ever done that? If so, how did it feel? If you haven't done it yourself, have you observed other people doing so? How did it affect your opinion of them, or of the situation?

Do you believe that there are times when it's important to be completely open, and times when it's not? How do you distinguish between the two?

"

[In the earliest times] people did not have thoughts, and did not want to have thoughts, that they were unwilling to show on their faces.

"

Seen in any of heaven's light, all the spirits in the hells appear in the form of their own evil. Each one is in fact an image of her or his evil, since for each individual the inner and outer natures are acting as a unit, and the deeper elements present themselves to view in the outer ones—in the face, the body, the speech, and the behavior. So you can tell what they are like by looking at them. In general, they are forms of contempt for others, threats against people who do not revere them; they are forms of various shadings of hatred, of various forms of vengefulness. Savagery and cruelty show through from within. When others praise them, though, or revere and worship them, their faces compose themselves and look almost happy and gratified.

—*Heaven and Hell* 553

Key Concept

If someone has said something to make you angry, it's easy to demonize them. But here we have examples of what real demons are like: full of hate and infused with a love of cruelty and revenge. While there are absolutely people like that in the world, when you're angry, it's easy to attribute those negative characteristics to someone who isn't really that way at all. Swedenborg would recommend that we use the same strategy in either situation: respond with love. People who are truly hateful won't be able to stand it, and those who are simply being misheard will have a chance to open up.

For Discussion or Reflection

How would you define real evil? What kinds of speech or actions would cross that line for you?

If you see hateful speech or attitudes on display, how do you usually respond to them? What has happened when you respond in that way? Did you wish afterward that you'd done something different?

People who have only a vague concept of the inner self and the outer self believe that it is the inner self that thinks and intends and the outer that speaks and acts as a result, since thinking and intending are internal activities, and speaking and acting are external. It should be borne in mind, though, that when we think intelligently and intend wisely, we are thinking and intending from a spiritual inner nature, but when we do not think intelligently and intend wisely we are thinking and intending from an earthly inner nature.

— *New Jerusalem* 42

Key Concept

In one of the previous passages in this chapter (page 30), we saw a flow: divine love expresses itself as our individual love, that individual love leads to feelings, feelings lead to thoughts, and from there we speak and act. Based on that description, it might be easy to assume that if someone is being negative or ignorant, it's a product of their inner nature. But in this passage, we see that there's a distinction between the inner self, which is the part that's connected to the Divine, and the outer self, which is focused on material concerns such as having enough food and having a place to live. Sometimes we act from that outer self rather than from our inner, divine self, even when that's not our intention.

For Discussion or Reflection

During the course of your day, pay attention to your thoughts. Which ones come from your outer self, and which ones come from your inner self? How can you tell? What does each type of thought tell you about yourself and the world around you?

What are some examples of divisive, or conflict-inducing, behavior that would come from a person's outer self rather than from their inner self? Do you think it's possible for someone to tell the difference between that sort of behavior and behavior driven by their true self?

The Lord wants us not only to think and talk about divine matters but also to try to figure them out so that we ourselves come to see whether they are true or not. As long as the purpose of this thought, speech, and reasoning is to see the truth, we can say that it is from the Lord within us.

—*Divine Providence* 219:3

Key Concept

This passage is describing matters of faith, but it could also apply to our interactions with others: if we think about the dynamics behind them with a genuine intent to understand the truth, we might not always come to the right answer, but we can rest assured that the very effort comes from a will to express the Divine.

For Discussion or Reflection

Is it easy to find the truth? Think about a time when you were in a conflict, either with an individual or as part of a group. What were the truths that each side believed? Looking back on that time, do you think you see those positions in the same way today?

PUTTING ASIDE EGO

We're all a mix of different drives and motivations, some good and some bad. Learning to stop ourselves when we're about to slide into a negative state of mind—and to empathize with others when they lose that battle within themselves—is an important part of finding peace.

Every evil looks to us like a simple unit. That is how we see hatred and vengefulness, theft and fraud, adultery and promiscuity, pride and arrogance, and the like. We do not realize that there are countless elements in every evil, more than there are fibers and vessels in the human body. An evil person is a miniature form of hell, and hell is made up of millions of individuals, each one in a form that is human even though it is grotesque. All the fibers and all the vessels in that person are inverted. Essentially, a spirit is an evil that looks to itself like a single entity, but there are as many elements in it as there are compulsions that arise from it. We are all our own good or our own evil from our heads to the soles of our feet. So if evil people are like this, we can see that each one is an evil made up of countless different things that are distinct varieties of evil, things we refer to as the compulsions of that evil.

It then follows that if we are to be reformed, the Lord has to repair and turn around all these elements in the sequence in which they occur, and that this cannot be accomplished except by the Lord's divine providence working step by step from the beginning of our lives to the end.

— *Divine Providence* 296

Key Concept

Every person is a complex blend of convictions and experiences and thoughts and emotions. Although Swedenborg often writes in absolute terms, we rarely encounter a person who is wholly good or wholly evil—or, to put it another way, who is motivated completely by either divine love or hellish hate.

If we can see that complexity within others, it's the first step to empathy and understanding. If we can see it within ourselves, it's the first step to setting our self-love aside and working toward a state of divine love.

For Discussion or Reflection

Think of a specific friend who you know quite well. What forms of self-love or love for the world do you see within them? Which do you think they have more or less of? What forms do you see in yourself? Which do you have more or less of?

What forms of love for others and love for the Divine do you see within your friend? How about within yourself? Does your friend have more or less of them than of the self-centered loves? How about you?

We cannot sense the compulsions that underlie our own evils. We are aware of their pleasures, but we give them little conscious thought because the pleasures seduce our thinking and distract our reflections. As a result, unless we discover from some other source that they are evil, we call them good and commit them freely, in accord with the reasoning of our thoughts. When we do this, we incorporate them into ourselves.

To the extent that we rationalize them as permissible, we enlarge the court of our ruling love, our life's love. Its "court" is made up of our compulsions, since they are like its servants and courtiers through which it governs the more outward activities that are its realm. The nature of the ruler determines the nature of the servants and courtiers, and the nature of the whole realm as well. If the ruler is a devil, the ruler's servants and courtiers will be forms of madness and the general populace will be all kinds of distortion. The servants (who are called "wise" even though they are insane) use imaginary constructs and arguments based on illusions to make the distortions seem true and to be accepted as true.

Is there any way to change the state of people like this except by banishing the evils from their outer self? This is how the compulsions that are inherent in our evils are banished. Otherwise, no exit is offered to the compulsions and they remain pent up like a city under siege or a sealed abscess.

— Divine Providence 113

Key Concept

If we start to examine our own motivations, we quickly start to see patterns in our behavior that could be called evil—selfishness, anger, judgment of others that leads to division and conflict, a focus on pursuit of money or power. We may even have rationalized them and made them a part of ourselves (see page 18). It's easy to think that we're familiar with all these things in ourselves, but here Swedenborg points out that we're often blind to our own faults. It isn't until these issues are somehow brought to our attention that we can start the work of rejecting our own negative behavior, and as we do so, other issues come to light. That's when we know that we've taken the first steps on the path of love.

For Discussion or Reflection

Swedenborg tells us in many places (including the next passage) that the only way we can truly see our own evils is with the Lord's help. What forms might that help take in our lives? Why do you think we cannot truly change on our own?

"

We cannot sense the compulsions
that underlie our own evils.
We are aware of their pleasures,
but we give them little conscious
thought because the pleasures
seduce our thinking and distract
our reflections.

"

The reason no one is reformed in a state of fear is that fear takes away our freedom and rationality, or our "freeness" and our "reasonableness." Love opens the inner reaches of the mind, but fear closes them; and when they are closed, we do very little actual thinking, being conscious then only of what is impinging on our feelings or our senses. All the fears that beset our minds are like this.

I have already explained [§104] that we have inner and outer processes of thought. Fear can never occupy our inner thought processes. These are always in freedom because they are in our life's love. Fear can occupy our outer thought processes, though, and when it does, it closes off the inner thought processes. Once they are closed, we are no longer able to act freely and rationally, so we cannot be reformed.

— *Divine Providence* 139:1–2

Key Concept

The outer thought processes that Swedenborg describes here comprise our everyday, conscious mind: the sum of all our thoughts, feelings, and experiences. The inner thought processes are our connection to God. We may not be aware of it, but when that connection is opened, divine love and wisdom are influencing us in little ways all the time.

That connection to God is pure love, and there's no room in that part of us for fear or hate. But being immersed in fear—as, for example, we might be when confronted by someone whose goals or beliefs seem to threaten our way of life—cuts us off from that connection. Just as hate creates a gulf between us and the Divine (see page 24), so does fear.

For Discussion or Reflection

What types of conflict might be grounded in fear? Have you ever been in a conflict or felt divided from someone based on a fear of your own?

Can you think of a time when another person's anger or unreasonable behavior might actually have been the result of fear?

Does the statement that "fear takes away our freedom and rationality" make you think differently about your past encounters with this emotion?

The Lord teaches good and loving actions in many passages in the Word. He teaches such actions in Matthew when he instructs us to be reconciled with our neighbor:

> If you bring your gift to the altar and in doing so remember that your brother or sister has something against you, leave your gift there in front of the altar. First be reconciled with your brother or sister, and then come and offer your gift. And be kind and generous to your adversary when you are both on the way [to court], to keep your adversary from turning you over to a judge, keep the judge from turning you over to an officer, and keep you from being thrown in prison. I tell you in truth, you will not be released until you have paid the last penny. (Matthew 5:23–26)

Being reconciled with our brother or sister is turning our backs on hostility, hatred, and vengefulness. We can see that this is turning our backs on these evils because they are sins.

— *Life* 73

Key Concept

If we think about what comes from having conflicts and divisions in our lives, it sheds a new light on this Bible passage. Conflict resolution isn't just about making peace with our neighbor; it's about having peace within ourselves so we can truly be in the presence of the Divine.

The first step to putting aside our self-love, Swedenborg tells us, is to recognize our own faults. Now we've come to the second step: reconciling with others.

For Discussion or Reflection

Are you in conflict with someone right now, in either a major or a minor way? Is there someone who you feel divided from on a fundamental level? Would you be willing to consider going and reconciling with them right now? How does that thought make you feel?

Some examples may help to show what conscience is. Suppose you have another's goods without the other knowing it and can therefore profit from them with no fear of the law or of loss of position or reputation. If you nevertheless return the goods to the other because the goods are not yours, you are someone who has a conscience; you are doing a good thing because it is good, and doing the right thing because it is right. Or suppose you are offered a government position but you know that someone else who also wants that position would be of greater benefit to your country than you would. If you let the other person have the position for the good of your country, you are someone who has a good conscience. A similar principle would apply in many other situations.

— New Jerusalem 136

Key Concept

Most people would probably describe conscience as that "little voice" in the back of your head that prompts you to do the right thing. Swedenborg says that conscience is actually one of the ways that divine love flows in through our inner mind. It is doing the right thing for its own sake. By following the promptings of our conscience, we bring ourselves closer to a loving state of mind, and that can affect everything that we do.

For Discussion or Reflection

In many cases, following your conscience is easy. You find a wallet on the street and return it to the person who dropped it. But what about giving up a job you really want because the other person is more qualified? That's a pretty deep exercise of conscience—especially if the person is someone who you don't get along with.

Have you ever heard that "little voice" of conscience while in conflict with someone else? If so, what did it tell you to do? Did you listen? Whether you did or not, what was the outcome?

The hardest battle of all, though, is with our love of being in control because of our sense of self-importance. If we overcome this, we have no trouble overcoming our other evil loves, because this is the head of them all.

— Divine Providence 146

Key Concept

Love of being in control can take a lot of forms. One obvious form is seeking out positions of authority—whether
it's in business, politics, religion, or even personal relation-
ships. But a love of being in control can also manifest itself
as a belief that we're right, that our opinion or our way of
doing things is the best, and that anyone who doesn't agree
is just misguided. Following a path of love means putting all
of that aside and being open to other perspectives. Even in
cases where we don't agree, making the effort to understand
where the other person is coming from can yield unexpected
rewards.

For Discussion or Reflection

What do you have strong opinions about? Why do those
particular issues make you feel that way?

If you like, try an exercise: Pick an issue that you're pas-
sionate about, or a pet peeve, or something that never fails
to make you angry. Then take some time to contemplate
the opposite view. How does it feel to do so? How do you
feel about people who have that opinion or engage in those
actions? Do you think you could put yourself in their shoes
for a period of time? Why or why not?

Fundamentally speaking, goodwill is wanting what is best for others. This desire resides in the inner self. When people of goodwill resist an enemy, punish a guilty person, or discipline evil people, clearly they do so through the medium of their outer selves. Therefore after the situation comes to an end, they go back to the goodwill that is in their inner selves. As much and as usefully as they can, they then wish the others well and benefit those others in a spirit of goodwill.

People who have genuine goodwill have a passion for what is good. In their outer selves that passion can look like rage and blazing anger, but it dies away and becomes calm as soon as their opponents come back to their senses. It is very different for people who have no goodwill. Their passion is a rage and a hatred that heat and ignite their *inner* selves.

— *True Christianity* 408

Key Concept

Here's a question that you might have had when thinking about harboring anger: What if the behavior you're upset about is harmful to other people? Is it wrong to be angry at people who steal, or cheat, or even murder?

According to Swedenborg, if we are good people, then it's normal to be angry when we see others hurt. The difference is that it's not a lasting anger—in other words, we don't hang onto it and make it a part of us, and we don't continue to judge or seek retaliation against the person. We feel the anger when the situation is upon us, and we let it go once it's past.

For Discussion or Reflection

What would anger motivated by love look like in another person? What about anger motivated by emotions like fear or hate? How would you tell the difference? How would you tell the difference between the two inside yourself?

Loving our neighbor is intending and doing good not only to neighbors, friends, and good people but also to strangers, enemies, and evil people. But we exercise goodwill in our dealings with the latter in different ways than we do in our dealings with the former. We exercise goodwill in our dealings with our neighbors and friends by benefiting them directly. We exercise goodwill in our dealings with our enemies and evil people by benefiting them indirectly through our warnings, corrective action, punishments, and therefore efforts to improve them.

— *True Christianity* 407

Key Concept

Being loving toward people you like is easy: you treat them well and show them that you care, you do little things to help them or make them feel better, and so on. Actions like that are equally appropriate (if not more so) for people who you don't get along with on a personal level. But what about people who are actively hateful toward others, or even those who are engaging in criminal acts?

Sometimes the loving thing to do is to try to stop them from going down a bad road. This could involve *not* helping someone whose goal is to harm or to be destructive; *not* encouraging vindictive or hateful thoughts or actions; and perhaps having to report on someone who's involved in a crime—even if that person is someone you care about. Sometimes going along with someone in order to avoid a fight with them isn't the best solution for either of you.

For Discussion or Reflection

Have you ever been in a situation where someone you love was heading down the wrong path, whether it was criminal activity, hurting people around them, or some other type of destructive behavior? Did you get involved? If so, what happened as a result?

As a society, what would be a loving response to crime in general?

EMBRACING DIVINE LOVE

Loving others can be hard to do . . . but it feels pretty
good when you get it right.

Since goodwill resides in the inner self, where benevolence is felt, and then extends into the outer self, where good actions occur, it follows that people's inner selves are what we should love; and we should love their outer selves on the basis of their inner selves. Therefore we are to love people according to the type of goodness they have inside. It is the goodness itself, then, that is actually our neighbor.

— *True Christianity* 410:1

Key Concept

Being loving toward people who frustrate us, or who seem to be actively working against us, or who hurt either us or people we care about, can seem like an impossible task. Here, Swedenborg gives us a way to help us get to such a place: while we can't see through to a person's inner self, we can look for the good qualities within them, and we can stay focused on those qualities when we're tempted to give in to our own negative emotions.

For Discussion or Reflection

Pick a person who you've been in conflict with or who regularly frustrates you. Can you name some good qualities about that person? What happens if you try to focus on loving those qualities? Do you think you would be able to hold on to that love in the midst of a frustrating moment?

Everyone is our neighbor, and people come in an infinite variety. Since we need to love them all as our neighbor for the type of goodness they possess, clearly there are genera and species of loving our neighbor, as well as higher and lower degrees of that love.

Since the Lord is to be loved above all else, it follows that the degrees of our love for our neighbors depend on their love for the Lord, that is, on the amount of the Lord or the amount from the Lord that our neighbors possess in themselves. That is also the amount of goodness they possess, since all goodness comes from the Lord.

Nevertheless, since these degrees are within people's inner selves and these are rarely obvious to the world, it is enough to love our neighbor by the degree of goodness that we are aware of.

— *True Christianity* 410:2–3

Key Concept

This starts out with a powerful proposition: "Everyone is our neighbor." No matter how bad they seem, no matter how you might be tempted to write them off and think that they don't have any redeemable qualities, everyone has something inside that you can love.

However, Swedenborg quickly brings us back to reality: there are degrees of love. You don't have to love everyone in the same way. Since we're human, and all we have is our own limited perception of reality, we tend to love according to that perception.

For Discussion or Reflection

Imagine the most unlovable person in the world. Maybe it's based on someone you know, or maybe it's a fictitious person. What is that person like? Is there a particular characteristic or type of behavior that you wouldn't be able to get past? If so, what is it, and why does that characteristic pose such a problem for you?

Do you agree that we should love others based on how much they love the Divine? If not, what do you think our love for others should be based on?

People often say, "I love such-and-such a person because that person loves me and does me good," but loving others for this reason alone is not loving them deeply, unless we ourselves are intent on what is good and love the good things that they do for that reason. That is being devoted to caring: the other is being focused on a kind of friendship that is not the same as caring.

When we love others because we care about them, we unite with the good they do and not with their personality, except insofar and as long as they are engaged in doing what is good. Then we are spiritual and are loving our neighbor spiritually. If we love others merely out of friendship, though, we unite ourselves with their personality, including the evil that belongs to them. In that case it is hard for us to separate ourselves after death from a personality that is devoted to evil, though in the former case, we can.

Caring makes this distinction by means of faith because faith is truth, and when through truth we are truly caring we look carefully and see what we should love; and when we are loving and benefiting others, we focus on the quality of usefulness in what we are doing.

— *Faith* 21

Key Concept

Here's an additional twist to the idea of loving your neighbor: If you love someone because of their personality, however wonderful that personality might be, you're not truly engaged in the type of love Swedenborg calls "charity" or "goodwill" (or, in the above passage, "caring"). On the other hand, if we love the goodness in a person, we're not only truly loving them but we're also uniting with them on a spiritual level.

For Discussion or Reflection

In the last two sections, we asked you to consider loving the good qualities in an individual whose personality you don't like. In this passage, we see that this type of love isn't just about empathy; it spiritually unites us with a person. How do you think it feels to be spiritually united with a person? How would you feel about being spiritually united with someone whose personality rubs you the wrong way?

Where neighborly love is absent, self-love is present, along with hatred for anyone who does not cater to oneself. That is why people who lack neighborly love see nothing in their neighbor besides that neighbor's evil. If they see anything good in the person, they either dismiss it or put a bad interpretation on it.

People governed by charity act in an entirely different way.

These differences form the distinction between the two types of people, particularly when they enter the other life. Those who lack all kindness radiate hatred from every pore. They want to examine and in fact judge everyone and crave nothing more than to find evil, constantly bent as they are on condemning, punishing, and torturing others.

Those who are guided by kindness, on the other hand, hardly even notice evil in another but pay attention instead to everything good and true in the person. When they do find anything bad or false, they put a good interpretation on it. This is a characteristic of all angels—one they acquire from the Lord, who bends everything bad toward good.

— *Secrets of Heaven* 1079:2

Key Concept

We have a tendency to look at others through the lens of our own love: if we tend to be hateful, or angry, or mistrustful, we expect others to be, too. A way to combat this tendency is to focus on the inner qualities of others, because that's where their goodness resides. Now, we're seeing the next step in this process: If we are good people, we look for the good in others, and we tend to overlook the bad or give it the best possible interpretation. And if we can do that, we can see the good in anything. This, Swedenborg tells us, is how angels view us.

For Discussion or Reflection

Do you know people who always see the best in others, who perhaps get accused of being too optimistic, or even naïve? Are you one of those people? Does the above passage make you think differently about that type of outlook on life?

If everyone were able to see bad or false qualities as good and true, what kind of place would the world be?

Bonus question: Do you think angels would leave their cars unlocked in a high-crime area?

Loving our neighbor as ourselves is simply not dealing dishonestly or unfairly with people, not harboring hatred or burning with revenge against them, not speaking ill of them or slandering them, not committing adultery with their spouses, and not doing anything of that nature to them. Can anyone fail to see that people who *do* do things like this are not loving their neighbor as themselves? However, people who do not do such things because they are both bad for their neighbor and sins against God treat their neighbor honestly, fairly, cordially, and faithfully. Since the Lord acts in the same way, a mutual union results.

When there is a mutual union, then whatever we do for our neighbor we do from the Lord, and whatever we do from the Lord is good.

— *Divine Providence* 94

Key Concept

Here, we learn a bit more about what it means to truly love others. Did you notice that some of the items on this list—for example, not slandering and not committing adultery—are taken straight from the Ten Commandments? That gives us a hint: looking for the good in others is certainly part of the process, but the commandments offer specific things that we can do to avoid conflicts and doing harm to others.

It may seem obvious to say that the Lord doesn't do those things either, but think for a moment about the implications: God doesn't hate people, or get angry, or seek revenge. How often do you come across the image of an angry God? Swedenborg not only tells us that the source of love can't be like that, but he also gives us the formula for union with the Lord.

For Discussion or Reflection

Has the belief in an angry or vengeful God ever been part of your spiritual practice? What do you think are the advantages or disadvantages to having such a belief? How do you react to the idea that God is able only to love people, no matter what they've done?

Anyone can grasp mentally and see rationally that to the extent that we resolutely abstain from theft and cheating, we love honesty, integrity, and justice. To the extent that we resolutely abstain from vengefulness and hatred, we love our neighbor. To the extent that we resolutely abstain from adultery, we love chastity, and so on.

However, hardly anyone knows what is heavenly and divine about honesty, integrity, justice, love for our neighbor, chastity, and the other desires of heavenly love until their opposites have been removed. Once their opposites have been removed, we are involved in them, so we recognize and see them from the inside. Until that happens, there is a kind of veil in the way. It does let a little of heaven's light reach our love, but since that love does not love wisdom, its spouse, to that extent, it does not accept the light.

— *Divine Love and Wisdom* 419

Key Concept

Once we begin the work of rejecting hatred and fear—even when we have a reason for feeling that way—we start to experience divine love to a greater and greater degree. And when we get that experience of divine love and joy, it becomes much easier for us to act on those emotions even in difficult situations. Swedenborg warns us not to get complacent, though; that state of mind can be hard to maintain, and when we fall back into our old way of thinking, it's easy to fool ourselves into thinking that we're still maintaining it.

For Discussion or Reflection

How do you think an experience of divine love feels? Have you had such an experience? If so, what conditions made this experience possible for you?

Most people have good and bad days—days when they are able to experience empathy or love for others, and days when that state feels very far away. Does that apply to you? If so, how do you deal with the bad days?

In the Christian world, it is doctrine that differentiates churches. Doctrine is the basis on which people call themselves Roman Catholic, Lutheran (or Evangelical), Calvinist (or Reformed), and other names as well. These names grow out of doctrine alone, which would never happen if we considered love for the Lord and charity for our neighbor the chief concern of faith. If we did, those distinctions would simply be differences of opinion on the mysteries of faith. True Christians would leave such issues up to the individual and the individual's conscience. In their hearts they would say, "A person who lives as a Christian—who lives as the Lord teaches—is a real Christian." One church would come out of all the different churches, and all disagreement due to doctrine alone would vanish. Even the hatred of one denomination for another would melt away in a moment, and the Lord's kingdom would come on earth.

— *Secrets of Heaven* 1799:4

Key Concept

Religion is one of the criteria that people often use to judge each other. In the time and place where Swedenborg lived, the deepest divisions were between different denominations of Christianity. In modern Western society, however, we see suspicion and mistrust of people of different religions, and we also see rifts between the religious and the non-religious. So we might wonder if Swedenborg's vision of a united humanity, one in which everyone made love the chief concern of their faith, could come about.

For Discussion or Reflection

Have you ever been in the middle of (or a witness to) a conflict between two or more people over the details of religious doctrine or interpretation? Thinking back over the previous discussions of the different types of love, in your experience, what was the love motivating each side? Did it seem as though they were capable of getting to a place where both of their loves could be fulfilled?

Do you think that someone who isn't religious can still act with love toward their neighbor? Could they have a love for the Divine, even if they don't believe in God? Why or why not?

THE BEAUTY IN VARIETY

Differences can often be a breeding ground for disagreement. But there's another way to look at it. What if what makes us different makes us better able to live in harmony with others?

Every perfect whole arises from a variety of elements, for a whole that is not composed of a variety of elements is not really anything. It has no form, and therefore no quality. However, when a whole does arise from a variety of elements, and the elements are in a perfected form in which each associates with the next in the series like a sympathetic friend, then it has a perfect quality. Heaven is, then, a single whole composed of a variety of elements arranged in the most perfect form; for of all forms, the form of heaven is the most perfect.

We can see that this underlies all perfection from every instance of beauty, charm, and delight that moves both our senses and our spirits. Such instances arise and flow invariably from a harmonious agreement of many things that are in sympathetic concord, whether they are together simultaneously or follow in a sequence. They do not flow from a single unit that lacks plurality. So we say that variety delights, and recognize that the delight depends on the quality of the variety.

— *Heaven and Hell* 56

Key Concept

Every perfect whole has variety within it. If all of the elements were the same, then the idea of wholeness would lose its meaning. Notice that there's no suggestion here that heaven is perfect because everyone is alike; rather, heaven is perfect because there are many people within it, each of whom makes their own unique contribution.

For Discussion or Reflection

Do you see beauty in variety in this world? If so, what are some examples of it?

As human beings, we also tend to see beauty in things that are the same, such as repeating patterns and symmetrical shapes. How would you compare that type of beauty to the examples of beauty that you just described?

How are diverse groups of people different from homogeneous groups of people? How do you imagine the answer would be different when describing heavenly communities versus describing communities on earth?

It is part of the divine design that things proceed from beginning to end; this is both a pattern overall and a pattern in smaller increments within the overall pattern. This design allows for the variety of all things, and this variety allows there to be qualities of all kinds. The quality of anything is more perfectly assessed through its contrast to things that are somewhat its opposite and things that are very much its opposite.

Darkness allows us to appreciate what a wonderful thing light is, and coldness allows us to appreciate what a wonderful thing heat is. Likewise (as everyone surely recognizes), falsity allows us to appreciate what a wonderful thing truth is, and evil allows us to appreciate what a wonderful thing goodness is.

— *True Christianity* 763

Key Concept

In an earlier passage (page 20), we saw that sometimes evil is allowed to happen so that we can see and understand more clearly what it is and what effects it has. As mixtures of both love and hate, our dark emotions can also help us to see the love inside us more clearly. Our dark days allow us to better appreciate the good ones.

Here, we see another benefit of the "dark side" of human nature: it allows us to better appreciate the good qualities we encounter in others, which in turn leads us into a more angelic state of mind.

For Discussion or Reflection

Think about something good in your life—something wonderful that makes you happy and sustains you through the tough times. What kinds of darkness help you better appreciate that light?

Now, think about something inside yourself that you'd like to change—a source of anger, fear, or hatred. What is its opposite? Do you have some of that opposite within you, too? Does contemplating that counterpart to your inner darkness shed "light" on your inner self?

People who are in the head in the universal human that is heaven are supremely involved in everything good. In fact, they are in love, peace, innocence, wisdom, intelligence, and therefore in delight and happiness. These flow into the head and into the components of the head in us, and correspond to them.

People who are in the chest of the universal human that is heaven are involved in the qualities of thoughtfulness and faith, and also flow into our chests and correspond to them. However, people who are in the groin of the universal human or heaven and in the organs dedicated to reproduction are in marriage love.

People who are in the feet are in the outmost heaven, which is called "natural-spiritual good." People who are in the arms and hands are in the power of what is true because of what is good. People who are in the eyes are in understanding; people who are in the ears are in attentiveness and obedience; people who are in the nostrils are in perception; people in the mouth and tongue in conversing from discernment and perception.

People who are in the kidneys are in truth that probes and discriminates and purifies; people in the liver, pancreas, and spleen are in various aspects of purification of what is good and true; and so on. They flow into the like parts of the human being and correspond to them.

The inflow of heaven is into the functions and uses of these members, and since the uses originate in the spiritual world, they take form by means of elements characteristic of the natural world and thus make themselves known in their effects. This is the origin of correspondence.

— Heaven and Hell 96

Key Concept

In the above passage, Swedenborg describes a number of different types of people and how they fit into the *universal human*—that is, the human structure of heaven. If there weren't such a variety of different types, heaven simply wouldn't work—it wouldn't be a perfect whole, as we saw earlier (page 82). And yet, not all of these people might be fun to be around. For example, a "kidney" person, who's always probing others to find out what's inside them and separating out the good from the bad, could be downright annoying at times. But each of these different types of people still has goodness within them, and each does their own part to make the world better.

For Discussion or Reflection

What part of the universal human do you think you would be in? Why?

What types of people do you get along with? What types do you not get along with? Where do you think they would fit into that greater human structure?

"

The diversity in created things
arises from the fact that there
are infinite things in the Divine-
Human One .

"

The diversity in created things arises from the fact that there are infinite things in the Divine-Human One and therefore unlimited things in that sun that is the first emanation from him, and those unlimited things emerge in the created universe as their reflections, so to speak. This is why there cannot be one thing identical to another anywhere. This is the cause of that variety of all things that meet our eyes in the context of space in this physical world, and in the appearance of space in the spiritual world. The variety is characteristic of both aggregates and details.

— *Divine Love and Wisdom* 155

Key Concept

Even though there is such diversity in the world—so many different types of animals and plants and minerals and things that can be made by combining different elements—everything that exists is still part of God. In fact, it's God's infinite nature that gives us this diversity of uniquenesses. As Swedenborg goes on to say later in *Divine Love and Wisdom* 155, "infinite things are distinguishably one in the Divine-Human One." So everything that exists reflects the Divine in some way.

For Discussion or Reflection

When we talk about "becoming one" with something, often we imagine the two things blending together until they're the same. How can everything be fundamentally the same at its core, and yet so different in expression? How do you visualize that dynamic?

Can a group of people still be united if there are differences between members? What about disagreements or outright conflict?

Another fact to be aware of is that no community can ever be completely and absolutely the same as another, and within a community, no individual can ever be exactly like another. To everything there is a concordant and harmonious variety. The Lord brings this variety into order in such a way that everything bends toward a common goal. This he accomplishes by means of our love for him and faith in him. The result is unity.

— *Secrets of Heaven* 690

Key Concept

In the past few passages, we've seen both the beauty and the importance of the uniqueness of every person and thing in creation. This variety doesn't happen by accident. It arises out of the infinite number of different aspects of the Divine. Not every being that came from God returns to God through love and faith, but the ones that do so become part of the divine pattern. In that moment, no matter how different we may seem, we are all united in a single whole.

For Discussion or Reflection

Have you ever had that sense of being united with others through divine love? If so, what was it like? If not, what do you imagine it would be like?

Think about a community that you're a part of. It could be with your family, at work, or with friends. What is your role within that community? What unique contribution do you make to its harmony?

In this passage, Swedenborg says that the Lord is bending everything toward a common goal. What do you think that goal is?

About Emanuel Swedenborg

*Emanuel Swedenborg (1688–1772) was born Emanuel Swed-*berg (or Svedberg) in Stockholm, Sweden, on January 29, 1688 (Julian calendar). He was the third of the nine children of Jesper Swedberg (1653–1735) and Sara Behm (1666–1696). At the age of eight, he lost his mother. After the death of his only older brother ten days later, he became the oldest living son. In 1697, his father married Sara Bergia (1666–1720), who developed a great affection for Emanuel and left him a significant inheritance. His father, a Lutheran clergyman, later became a celebrated and controversial bishop whose diocese included the Swedish churches in Pennsylvania and in London, England.

After studying at the University of Uppsala (1699–1709), Emanuel journeyed to England, Holland, France, and Germany (1710–1715) to study and work with leading scientists in Western Europe. Upon his return, he apprenticed as an engineer under the brilliant Swedish inventor Christopher

Polhem (1661–1751). Emanuel gained favor with Sweden's King Charles XII (1682–1718), who gave him a salaried position as an overseer of Sweden's mining industry (1716–1747). Although he was engaged, he never married.

After the death of Charles XII, Emanuel was ennobled by Queen Ulrika Eleonora (1688–1741), and his last name was changed to Swedenborg (or Svedenborg). This change in status gave him a seat in the Swedish House of Nobles, where he remained an active participant in the Swedish government throughout his life.

As a member of the Royal Swedish Academy of Sciences, Emanuel devoted himself to scientific studies and philosophical reflections that culminated in a number of publications, most notably a comprehensive three-volume work on mineralogy (1734) that brought him recognition across Europe. After 1734, he redirected his research and publishing to a study of anatomy in search of the interface between the soul and body. He made several significant discoveries in physiology.

During a transitional phase from 1743 to 1745, Emanuel shifted his main focus from science and philosophy to theology. Throughout the rest of his life, he maintained that this shift was brought about by Jesus Christ, who appeared

to him, called him to a new mission, and opened his perception to a permanent dual consciousness of this life and the
life after death.

Emanuel devoted the last decades of his life to studying Scripture and publishing eighteen theological titles that
draw on the Bible, reasoning, and his own spiritual experiences. These works present a Christian theology with unique
perspectives on the nature of God, the spiritual world, the
Bible, the human mind, and the path to salvation.

Emanuel Swedenborg died in London on March 29,
1772, at the age of eighty-four.

ooooo

Sources

Quotes from Emanuel Swedenborg's writings were taken from the New Century Edition of the Works of Emanuel Swedenborg, as follows:

Divine Love and Wisdom, trans. George F. Dole
(West Chester, PA: Swedenborg Foundation, 2010, 2015)

Divine Providence, trans. George F. Dole
(West Chester, PA: Swedenborg Foundation, 2010, 2017)

Heaven and Hell, trans. George F. Dole
(West Chester, PA: Swedenborg Foundation, 2010, 2016)

Life / Faith, trans. George F. Dole
(West Chester, PA: Swedenborg Foundation, 2014)

New Jerusalem, trans. George F. Dole and Jonathan S. Rose
(West Chester, PA: Swedenborg Foundation, 2016)

Other Planets, trans. George F. Dole and Jonathan S. Rose
(West Chester, PA: Swedenborg Foundation, 2018)

Secrets of Heaven, trans. Lisa Hyatt Cooper, vols. 1–2
(West Chester, PA: Swedenborg Foundation, 2010, 2012)

True Christianity, trans. Jonathan S. Rose, vols. 1–2
(West Chester, PA: Swedenborg Foundation, 2010, 2011, 2017)